Teaching the Novels of
Gary Paulsen

by Howard Gutner

SCHOLASTIC
PROFESSIONAL BOOKS

New York • Toronto • London • Auckland • Sydney
Mexico City • New Delhi • Hong Kong

Cover design by Norma Ortiz

Cover illustration by Mona Mark

Interior design by Sydney Wright

ISBN 0-439-09840-8

Contents

Introduction 5

Unit One

WOODSONG

Synopsis 11
Setting a Purpose for Reading 11
Comprehension Strategy: Cause and Effect .12
Literary Element: Setting 12
Vocabulary 13

Comprehension Questions 14
Exploring Cause and Effect . Graphic Organizer .16
Exploring Setting 17
Writing Activities 18
Group and Individual Classroom Projects . .19

DOGSONG

Synopsis 20
Setting a Purpose for Reading 20
Literary Element: Theme 21
Literary Element: Character 22
Vocabulary 22

Comprehension Questions 23
Exploring Theme 25
Exploring Character . . . Graphic Organizer 26
Writing Activities 27
Group and Individual Classroom Projects . .28

Unit Discussion Questions 29

Unit Two

HATCHET

Synopsis 30
Setting a Purpose for Reading 31
Literary Element: Plot 31
Literary Element: Mood 31
Vocabulary 32

Comprehension Questions 33
Exploring Plot . . . . Graphic Organizer 35
Exploring Mood 36
Writing Activities 37
Group and Individual Classroom Projects . .38

THE RIVER

Synopsis 39
Setting a Purpose for Reading 40
Comprhension Strategy: Summary 40
Literary Element: Author's Language 41
Vocabulary 41

Comprehension Questions 42
Exploring Summary . . . Graphic Organizer 44
Exploring Author's Language 45
Writing Activities 46
Group and Individual Classroom Projects . .47

BRIAN'S WINTER

Synopsis 48
Setting a Purpose for Reading 48
Comprehension Strategy: Sequence 49
Literary Element: Tone 49
Vocabulary 50

Comprehension Questions 51
Exploring Sequence . . . Graphic Organizer 53
Exploring Tone . . . . . . Graphic Organizer 54
Writing Activities 55
Group and Individual Classroom Projects . .56

Unit Discussion Questions 57

Answer Key 58

Introduction

Gary Paulsen and the Search for Meaning

The search for meaning and a system of values in the harsh natural world has been a feature of much American literature, from Hemingway's *The Macomber Affair* to Norman Maclean's *A River Runs Through It*. Gary Paulsen has addressed this topic in a series of over 20 novels for young adults, as his characters face a direct struggle with nature and, at the same time, learn valuable lessons about the interrelationships between people and animals. "I understood almost nothing about the woods until it was nearly too late," Paulsen writes in the opening sentence of *Woodsong*, a thrilling autobiographical account of his training sessions with a team of sled dogs for the Alaskan Iditarod. "I knew that somewhere in the dogs, in their humor and the way they thought, they had great, old knowledge; they had something we had lost. And the dogs could teach me."

In addition to the struggles and learning experiences his characters encounter as they go head-to-head with nature, many of Gary Paulsen's books are inspired by common characteristics that stem from his own personal understanding of the natural world. The trilogy *Hatchet*, *The River*, and *Brian's Winter*, for example, take place in a Canadian wilderness that bears a close resemblance to the deep Minnesota woods where Paulsen spent many years. His experiences training for the Iditarod not only led him to the breathtaking drama of his own story, *Woodsong*, but also to the fictional tale of a 14-year-old Eskimo boy in *Dogsong*.

Each of these titles fuses the conflict of people versus nature with the conflict of man versus himself, in an exciting interplay of the mystical and the real. One reason for Paulsen's continuing popularity among young adults is his ability to create narratives that show teen protagonists living life as a challenge—a striking contrast to much of the current realistic fiction for teens and pre-teens, in which characters must cope with their existence within an urban landscape over which they have little control. This book aims to help your students recognize the similarity of themes and literary elements at work in Paulsen's writing. Students can then utilize what they have learned as they read other titles—both by Paulsen and by other authors who work in different genres.

How the Novels are Presented

The five novels chosen for study in this book have been selected to illustrate certain themes and elements that appear again and again in Paulsen's work. Each novel is presented for the whole class to study either together or in small groups.

Woodsong and *Dogsong* are paired in the first unit because they each deal with rigorous journeys of self-discovery. *Hatchet*, *The River*, and *Brian's Winter* form a trilogy in the second unit because they each feature the same protagonist, 13-year-old Brian Robeson. In the first two novels, Brian must rely on his intelligence and instincts to survive when he is stranded in the Canadian wilderness. *The River* takes Brian back to the wilderness after his rescue, at the request of a government survival school. Students will have an opportunity to study each book individually and then compare the works in each unit for similarities in both theme and literary element.

Teaching Options

Complete flexibility is a key feature of *Teaching the Novels of Gary Paulsen*, a study guide that offers a number of options for instruction. The two units that comprise the guide are independent of one another, so that you may elect to do one or both units as your classroom time permits. Further, if you elect to omit the Unit Discussion Questions, each individual novel can also be taught independently.

In each lesson in this study guide, you will find a synopsis of the novel. Following the synopsis, questions are provided to assist you in helping your students set a purpose for reading. Literary elements, as well as comprehension strategies, are highlighted to increase your students' understanding of each novel. Whole-group vocabulary development activities focus on story words that are organized around a central concept. ESL strategies reinforce second-language learners' comprehension of words and phrases that relate to specific concepts in the story. Through reproducibles, including graphic organizers, students will have the opportunity to reinforce what they have learned about the specific literary elements and comprehension strategies studied. In addition, reproducible comprehension questions will assess students' reading for aesthetic response, critical analysis, and an understanding of character and plot development. Finally, you have your choice of four writing activities and four classroom projects for each novel. These are built around a succession of disciplines—including math, social studies, language arts, geography, art, and science—giving you options to extend your students' learning and providing them with ways to make meaning from the text of each book.

Additional Resources:
Related Reading, Audiotapes, and Web Sites

Books for Students
George, Jean Craighead. *My Side of the Mountain*. New York: Dutton Books, 1988.
George, Jean Craighead. *Julie of the Wolves*. New York: HarperCollins, 1972.
London, Jack. *The Call of the Wild*. New York: Scholastic, 1988.
North, Sterling. *The Wolfling*. New York: Scholastic, 1980.
Paulsen, Gary. *Brian's Return*. New York: Delacorte Press, 1999.
Paulsen, Gary. *The Voyage of the Frog*. New York: Bantam Doubleday Dell, 1996.
Sperry, Armstrong. *Call It Courage*. New York: Scholastic, 1995.

Books for Teachers
Paulsen, Gary. *Eastern Sun, Winter Moon*. New York: Harvest Books, 1995.
Savner, Gary M. *Presenting Gary Paulsen*. New York: Macmillan, 1996.

Books on Audiotape
Woodsong, *Hatchet*, *The River*, and *Brian's Winter* are all available on audiotape from Bantam Books. *Dogsong* is available on audiotape from Ballantine.

Gary Paulsen Web Sites
http://www.garypaulsen.com
The author's official Web site. Includes a letter from Paulsen, continuously updated, about his latest adventures; pictures from his latest book tour; a complete bibliography; a biography; and a link that allows students to submit their questions directly to the author.

http://members.aol.com/goal1/paulsen.html
A Gary Paulsen Web site created by the fourth-grade students in Mrs. Granchelli's class in Medina, New York. Includes links to other Gary Paulsen sites, as well as an opportunity to e-mail students in Granchelli's class to exchange views and opinions on Paulsen.

http://www.scils.rutgers.edu/special/kay/paulsen.html
This Web site, entitled "Learning About Gary Paulsen," features a biography, a complete list of literary awards the author has won, reviews, and a number of links for more information on Paulsen.

http://teacher.scholastic.com/iditarod/paulsen.htm
This URL will take you to Scholastic's home page on the Iditarod. Its links feature teaching suggestions, ideas for cross-curricular activities, and an extensive interview with Gary Paulsen.

About Gary Paulsen

Gary Paulsen was born on May 17, 1939, in Minneapolis, Minnesota. His father, Oscar, was a career army officer who served on General Patton's staff during World War II. "I was an 'army brat,' and it was a miserable life," Paulsen has written about his childhood. "We moved around constantly. School was a nightmare because I was unbelievably shy, and terrible at sports."

His home life was barely an improvement. Both parents were alcoholics and often fought. Eventually, Paulsen was sent to live with his grandmother and aunts.

As a teenager living in northern Minnesota, Paulsen sold newspapers on a street corner after school to make extra money. On one particularly cold evening, he was walking home after selling the last of his papers when he passed the public library. Paulsen could see the reading room bathed in a beautiful golden light.

"I went in to get warm," Paulsen recalls, "and the librarian asked me if I wanted something. I said no, I just wanted to warm up a little. And then she said, 'Do you want a library card?' So I said yeah. She handed me a card with my name on it—my name—which was amazing to me. And then she asked if I wanted a book. I said, 'Sure,' kind of cocky. And she said to bring it back when I was done and she'd give me another one. This went on for a long time. The librarian kept giving me books; at first it took me a month to read a book, then two weeks, then a week, and pretty soon I was reading two books a week. She'd give me Westerns and science fiction, and every once in a while she'd schlepp in a Melville. It saved me, it really did. And I don't think any of the good things that have happened to me would have been possible without that librarian and libraries in general."

After attending Bemidji College for a year, Paulsen left school and served in the army for three years, attaining the rank of sergeant. Upon leaving the service, he took extension courses and became a field engineer. "I was good at my work, but didn't like it," he says now. "One day I read a magazine article on flight testing a new airplane and thought, what a way to make a living—writing about something you like and getting paid for it."

Although he had no publishing experience, Paulsen soon left his job in engineering and went to work for a men's magazine in California. "They could see I was serious about wanting to learn," he says now, "and they were willing to teach me. We published some excellent writers—Steinbeck, Bradbury, Ellison—which was great training and exposure for me."

In 1966, Paulsen's first book was published, a memoir of his tour of duty in Vietnam entitled *The Special War*. It would be the first of many books in which Paulsen drew on real-life experiences to shape his written narrative, and those experiences would multiply as time passed. Returning to his native Minnesota in the late 1960s, Paulsen worked as a hunter and trapper, and in the early 1970s became a two-time competitor in the Iditarod, an Alaskan dogsled race that covers about 1,200 miles. Paulsen used these experiences to write a series of novels and memoirs that tap into what he knows best—the interplay between people and animals, and human survival in the wilderness against incredible odds. His firsthand knowledge comes through clearly in the descriptive details he uses, making the reader feel as if he or she is a part of the story.

"My life is an adventure story," Paulsen has said. "Everything I write about is based on things I've lived. I've been in two forced landings, like in *Hatchet*. I've hunted in the bush. Or the Iditarod books—I've raced. Part of it is, so very few books are being written for boys. Now, it has crossed over. I get 400 letters a day, and half are from boys, half from girls."

Paulsen has won more than 50 awards for his juvenile fiction, including three Newbery Honor citations for the novels *Dogsong*, *Hatchet*, and *The Winter Room*. In addition, *Dogsong* received a Child Study Association of America award.

Learning magazine named Paulsen's novel *The Voyage of the Frog* a Best Book of the Year, and *Parenting* magazine bestowed a similar honor on *The Winter Room*. *Hatchet* won a Booklist Editor's Choice citation in 1988, and the Western Writers of America gave Paulsen their Spur Award for *Woodsong* and *The Haymeadow*. In 1994, the IRA/Children's Book Council named the novels *Dogsong* and *Nightjohn* Children's Choice books. *Brian's Winter*, an IRA Young Adults' Choice for 1997, has also been named to a number of Master Reading Lists for young people in the states of Nebraska, Indiana, Wyoming, South Carolina, and Iowa. *The River* was named Best Book of the Year by *Parents* magazine and is also an IRA Children's Choice.

"It's like things have come full circle," Paulsen says. "I felt like nothing the first time I walked into a library, and now library associations are giving me awards. It means a lot to me."

Gary Paulsen has been married three times and is the father of three children. His current wife, the former Ruth Ellen White, is an artist who has illustrated many of his books. Today the Paulsens live on a ranch in La Luz, New Mexico, while maintaining a second home in Minnesota and a sailboat in California.

Woodsong

Synopsis

In *Woodsong*, a spare but thrilling autobiographical account of a series of adventures that changed his life, Gary Paulsen relates how he arrived at a new understanding of the beauty, violence, and mystery of the natural world when he began training and running a pack of sled dogs. Although clearly drawn from the details of his life in the Minnesota wilderness, *Woodsong* is a series of reflections on the changes that took place in Paulsen's life rather than a day-to-day account presented in a chronological time frame.

In the opening section, Paulsen watches helplessly from his sled as a doe is caught and eaten by a pack of wolves. Confronted for the first time by the savagery of nature, he suddenly realizes that animals are not right or wrong, good or bad; they just "are." Shortly afterward, his favorite sled dog starts bleeding profusely during a night run. The dog survives, seemingly unconcerned by the experience, but Paulsen realizes how little he knows about animals and the forces that drive them. Finally, a "joke" one dog plays on another brings the author to the realization that dogs are highly intelligent. After these experiences he decides to stop hunting and trapping wild animals. His decision is reinforced when he is injured during a run and rescued from almost certain death by his team of dogs.

As Paulsen runs with his dogs in the Minnesota wilderness, he experiences a number of mysteries that he has never been able to solve, among them the source of a green light encountered during a midnight run, and a standing doe that has inexplicably frozen to death in the middle of a forest trail. The mysteries serve not only to deepen the author's awe of nature but also the growing realization of his own limitations as "just another animal in the woods."

On run after run, Paulsen slowly learns to trust his dogs and follow their lead. The book concludes with Paulsen's account of the Iditarod, a dogsled race he entered with his team that begins in Anchorage, Alaska, and ends in Nome—almost 1,200 miles.

Setting a Purpose for Reading

Invite students to skim the book and to read the synopsis on the inside dust jacket or on the back of the book. Students might then wish to set their own purposes for reading, or you can suggest the following:

1 Why do you suppose Gary Paulsen chose to call this book *Woodsong*? What do you think the "song of the woods" might be?

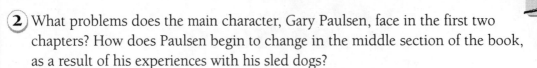

2 What problems does the main character, Gary Paulsen, face in the first two chapters? How does Paulsen begin to change in the middle section of the book, as a result of his experiences with his sled dogs?

3 What lessons does Paulsen learn from the woods as he takes his sled dogs on runs through the Minnesota wilderness?

4 What is the greatest challenge Paulsen faces during the Iditarod?

Comprehension Strategy: Cause and Effect

Point out to students that a cause is an event or action that makes another event or action occur. An effect is the direct or logical outcome of an event or action. Discuss with students how recognizing cause-and-effect situations when they read will enable them to understand how specific events, actions, occurrences, and character motives in a book can cause other events to occur. After students read the back cover copy, ask them what caused Gary Paulsen to decide to enter the Iditarod. (He traveled with his sled dogs through the Minnesota wilderness and enjoyed the experience.) Then discuss how an effect may become a cause, resulting in a cause-and-effect chain of events.

As students read, have them pay close attention to events in the book that cause other events to happen. Point out that one event in the plot can sometimes cause more than one other event to take place, resulting in a cause with multiple effects. Explain that keeping track of cause-and-effect situations in a book like *Woodsong* can help them understand the main character's behavior, and how and why he changes throughout the book. Suggest that as they read, students keep track of cause-and-effect situations on a chart like the one below:

WOODSONG

Cause	Effect

Literary Element: Setting

Remind students that the setting of a book, whether it is fiction or nonfiction, is the time and place in which the action occurs. Before students begin reading the novel on their own, call on a volunteer to read the paragraph near the beginning of Chapter 1, in which the author clearly establishes the principal setting of the book. The paragraph begins with the sentence "It was a grandly beautiful winter morning." After students have listened to the paragraph, discuss with them how the author paints the setting in a positive light. Then ask them to suggest some possible negative aspects of a winter setting in the deep woods of northern Minnesota. Record students' responses on a chart like the example provided on page 13.

SETTING DETAILS

Positive	Negative
Invigorating to both humans and dogs	Extreme cold
Bright sun	Danger of frostbite
Everything seems to sparkle	Danger of freezing to death

Have students pay close attention to the positive and negative aspects of the setting as they continue to read the book, and to how the setting changes once Paulsen arrives in Alaska to compete in the Iditarod. In addition, have students note how aspects of the setting influence cause-and-effect events throughout the book.

Vocabulary

Use a concept map to help students understand concept words related to the wilderness. Draw a circle with the word *wilderness* in the middle. Then build the map by drawing lines connecting the circled words or phrases *animals*, *dog sledding*, *weather*, and *the land* to the circle in the middle. Write story vocabulary on the board, such as *gangline*, *foraging*, *predator*, *prey*, *pelt*, *brindle wolf*, *temperature inversion*, *ruffled grouse*, *terrain*, *instinct*, and *stashes*, and have students suggest where each word should be placed on the map. If students need help, have volunteers look up the words in a dictionary. Students can also suggest additional categories and vocabulary words from the story to add to the concept map.

ESL Students whose first language is not English may benefit from listening to the audiotape of *Woodsong* (Bantam Books Audio, 1991) as they read along in the text. Words that relate specifically to dog sledding and the setting of the story—the environments of northern Minnesota and Alaska—may present problems for ESL students. Where possible, define the following terms for students and provide them with illustrations for each definition:

gangline a long rope to which a number of dogs are harnessed when they pull a sled

predator animal or person that lives by preying on other animals

gully a small, narrow valley

kennel a house for a dog or a group of dogs

streambed the sandy or muddy bottom of a stream where water flows

hibernation the act of sleeping through the winter

UNIT ONE

Comprehension Questions

Chapters 1–3

1 What effect did Gary Paulsen's observation of the doe's death have on him? How did it change the way he thought about the woods and the animals that live there?

_____

_____

_____

2 How and why does Paulsen begin running a team of dogs?

_____

_____

3 Why does Gary Paulsen stop hunting and trapping animals in the woods? In what way did his three "lessons in blood" affect his decision?

_____

_____

_____

4 Compare Paulsen's dogs Columbia and Olaf. Which one would you rather have pulling your sled? Why?

_____

_____

Chapters 4–6

5 What does Gary Paulsen see as the main difference between people and animals?

_____

6 What lesson about the woods did Paulsen learn from Scarhead the bear?

_____

7 Why did Hawk, the banty hen, turn the Paulsens' backyard into a "war zone"?

_____

_____

8 Name three "mysteries" that Paulsen encounters in the Minnesota woods.

_____

_____

_____

UNIT
ONE

Comprehension Questions

Chapters 7–8

1 What lesson do Cookie and the other dogs teach Paulsen?

_____

_____

_____

2 What is the significance of the stick that Storm carries in his mouth?

_____

_____

3 Why does Paulsen begin to hallucinate on one of his night runs with the dogs?

_____

The Race

4 Why did Paulsen enter the Iditarod? Do you think winning the race was important to him? Why or why not?

_____

_____

_____

5 Why does Paulsen lose control of the sled at the very beginning of the Iditarod?

_____

_____

6 What makes "The Burn" a very difficult part of the race?

_____

_____

7 Paulsen "meets" many strange people when he hallucinates during the race. In what ways are these people similar? How are they different?

_____

_____

_____

8 What do you think is the most difficult part of the Iditarod for Paulsen? Explain your answer.

_____

_____

_____

GRAPHIC ORGANIZER

Exploring Cause and Effect

An event in a story can have more than one effect. In Chapter 2 of *Woodsong*, Gary Paulsen gives his sled dogs dried food, and this causes one of the dogs to spray blood. But it also has an effect on Paulsen. He realizes after this event that he wants to learn all he can about dogs and about running a team. On the chart below, list some events from *Woodsong* and the effects they had, both on the plot and on Gary Paulsen.

Cause	Effect on Plot	Effect on Gary Paulsen
1		
2		
3		
4		

UNIT ONE

Exploring Setting

The setting of a story is where and when it takes place. The setting can change over the course of a book, and it is important because it can affect the characters in a story, their actions, and what happens to them. As you read *Woodsong*, note how the setting affects the plot and the characters in the book.

Beginning of the Book

1 What are the details that tell where this part of the story takes place?

_____

2 What are the details that tell when this part of the story takes place?

_____

3 How does the setting at the beginning of the book affect the plot?

_____

_____

_____

4 How does the setting at the beginning of the book affect Gary Paulsen?

_____

_____

_____

_____

End of the Book

1 What are the details that tell where this part of the story takes place?

_____

2 What are the details that tell when this part of the story takes place?

_____

3 How does the setting at the end of the book affect the plot?

_____

_____

_____

4 How does the setting at the end of the book affect Gary Paulsen?

_____

_____

_____

Writing Activities

Choose from among the following writing activities to inspire connections to *Woodsong*, as well as your students' imaginations.

Victory Speech

Remind students that when Gary Paulsen crosses the Iditarod finish line in Nome all he was able to say to the mayor, who greeted him, was "We'll be back to run it again." Invite students to imagine that they have not only finished the Iditarod but have claimed victory. Have them prepare a victory speech graciously accepting the prize and acknowledging the achievement. Instruct students to make their speeches three minutes long, and encourage them to describe at least one major problem that was overcome during the race. Also suggest that they acknowledge their lead dog and anyone who provided assistance along the way.

Journal Entry

Ask students to put themselves in Gary Paulsen's place as he runs with his sled dogs at the beginning of the book. Have them imagine that they are circling the lake with the team when suddenly the doe flies out of the woods, with the wolves close behind her. What would their reaction be? Would they try to intervene in some way? Have students write a journal entry in which they describe their reaction to this experience and what might be the result.

Mysteries of Nature

Review the "mysteries" of the woods that Paulsen describes in Chapter 6: The strange doe, frozen in the middle of the trail; the mysterious green light; the cedar waxwings passing berries from one to the other; and the fox that "could not have been there and yet was." Have students write their own explanations or solutions to one of these "mysteries" of nature.

Exploring Character

Point out to students that when Gary Paulsen describes the dogs he has owned, he gives each one a distinct personality. Some are extremely intelligent, and others have a great sense of humor. Have students write a character sketch of a favorite pet or a wild animal they have observed at home, in a zoo, or in a natural setting.

UNIT ONE

Group and Individual
Classroom Projects

Choose from among the following cross-curricular activities to enhance your students' understanding of the literature selections.

Art

Gary Paulsen's vivid descriptions in *Woodsong* easily lend themselves to artistic interpretation. Suggest that students use Paulsen's descriptions to illustrate several settings in the book, such as "The Burn" in Alaska or his home in the north woods of Minnesota. You may wish to suggest that students use details from the book to label the details in their pictures. Students can also use their illustrations as prompts to retell a section of the book.

Geography

Have students work in small groups to research and create a map of the Iditarod route in Alaska. The official Iditarod Web site provides details about towns and rest stops along the route as well as natural sights such as mountain ranges and valleys. Students may want to create an accompanying list of information about stops along the way. For example, the town of Knik is 63 miles into the route and has a population of 631. After this town, the teams head into the wilderness.

Social Studies

Invite students to research the history of sled dogs. Prior to the formal sport of sled dog racing, sled dogs were bred solely for the purpose of assisting native peoples of the Arctic region in tasks essential to their everyday survival. The two dogs commonly used in sledding, Alaskan Malamutes and Siberian Huskies, had different origins and uses. Alaskan Malamutes, originating with a group of Eskimo people known as the Mahlemiut, were very large freighting dogs. The Gold Rush in 1896 created a high demand for these dogs. Siberian Huskies, originating with the Chuckchi people of northeastern Siberia, were smaller and faster than their Mahlemiut counterparts.

Language Arts

Remind students that Paulsen reveals several mushing terms in *Woodsong*, such as *gee* and *haw*. Have students work in small groups to make and illustrate a dictionary of mushing terms. They can check sites on the Web for sledding terms, as well as books such as *Dog Driver* by Miki and Julie Collins (Alpine Publications, 1991), which features an extensive reference section with sledding terms. Encourage students to note the origins of as many words as possible. For example, the word *mush* comes from the French word *marche*, a form of the verb *marcher*, which means "to walk."

Dogsong

Synopsis

"I wrote *Dogsong* in camp while I was training my team for my first Iditarod," Gary Paulsen once noted, many years after the book had been published. "It'd be twenty below, and there I'd sit by the fire writing longhand in my notebook." *Dogsong* and *Woodsong* are companion pieces, each propelled by the exhilaration of running a dog team. However, *Woodsong* is an autobiographical account of dog sledding; *Dogsong* is realistic fiction. From the very first page, when we meet 14-year-old Russel Suskitt getting out of bed in the morning, the reader enters into his life and thoughts. And as we accompany him on his journey of self-discovery across the Arctic tundra, the strangeness of his Eskimo customs and environment fade into familiarity.

In the opening chapters, when Russel feels dissatisfied with his life in a government-built Eskimo village, his father advises him to speak with Oogruk, an old man who remembers the old Eskimo traditions. Oogruk tells Russel many stories about the old days, when each man "had his own song." Inspired by Oogruk's stories, Russel then becomes determined to find his own song. He takes Oogruk's sled and dogs out for short runs in the Arctic wilderness. Slowly, as he learns how to run the dogs and use the old Eskimo weapons to hunt, Russel begins to identify the beginnings of his song.

Then Oogruk asks Russel to take him out to the sea ice, and it becomes clear that he wants to die. Although he feels deeply conflicted over the old man's request, Russel obeys his wish, and then sets out on his own journey of self-discovery. He and the dogs become one, relying on each other for survival. One night Russel dreams about a hunter who kills a woolly mammoth to feed his family. He recognizes the hunter as himself, and the dream folds in and out of Russel's real life as he pushes the dogs farther north. When he finds an Eskimo girl his age, half-dead and pregnant in the midst of the wilderness, Russel nurses her back to health, and his song becomes complete.

Setting a Purpose for Reading

Invite students to skim the book and to read the synopsis on the inside dust jacket or on the back cover of the book. You may want to discuss with them the environment in which Eskimos live, above the Arctic Circle in northern Canada, Alaska, Siberia, and Greenland. Point out the region on a map, and share with students the following information: The sun doesn't set for six months of the year in this region, and for the other six months it never rises. The area is sparsely settled and extremely cold. Students might then wish to set their own purposes for reading, or you can suggest the following:

1. Why do you suppose Gary Paulsen called this book *Dogsong*? How will the sled dogs in this book help the main character, Russel Suskitt, find his own "song"?

2. What do you want to learn about Eskimo life and traditions from reading *Dogsong*?

3. What message about life or nature does Gary Paulsen want readers to come away with after reading *Dogsong*?

4. What does Russel Suskitt learn about himself on his journey with a dog team?

Literary Element: Theme

Explain to students that the theme of a story is a general, declarative statement that does not make reference to characters or events from the book. It is the message about life or nature that the author wants the reader to take away from the story. Point out that sometimes the author states the message directly in the text, but more often the theme is not stated directly. By recognizing the theme of a story, a reader will better understand the relationships between characters, events, and outcome, and will also develop a better understanding of what an author thinks or how the author feels about the story.

Present students with a strategy for identifying the theme in a story as they read. Discuss the following steps, which may be written on a chart or poster:

1. Think about what the characters do and say.

2. Think about what happens to the characters.

3. Ask yourself: What does the author want you to know about Russel Suskitt and his journey of self-discovery?

Students can compile their information on a chart like the one below:

What the Characters Do and Say		What Happens to the Characters
	+	

=

How the Author Feels About the Story

Literary Element: Character

Explain to students that a character in a story can be a person or an animal and that a character's traits are the special and more permanent qualities of a character's personality. In addition, what a character says, does, thinks, and feels are an expression of a character's personality.

As students read *Dogsong*, have them pay particular attention to Russel's character traits, as well as his feelings, which affect what he thinks, says, and does. Encourage them to note how these feelings are different from the character's more permanent traits, and to use these lasting traits as well as Russel's feelings to help them make predictions about his actions. Finally, point out that an author may reveal a character's traits and feelings by the way other characters talk about and act toward him or her. Suggest that students note how other characters in *Dogsong* react to Russel and how their reactions help to reveal his character.

Vocabulary

Use word webs to help students understand concept words related to Eskimo culture and the Arctic. Draw two circles, one titled "Eskimo Life," and the other "Arctic." Then build each web by adding the words *breechclout, muktuk, taggle, toggle, lance, gaggle, quiver, shaman, harpoon*, and *mukluk* around the circle labeled "Eskimo Life," and *ptarmigan, herds, caribou*, and *carcass* around the circle labeled "Arctic." As they read, have students use context clues to define the words on the web. Encourage them to pay close attention to words they encountered previously in *Woodsong*.

ESL Vocabulary related to Eskimo life and the Arctic may be difficult for students whose first language is not English. If your students are studying *Dogsong* as part of the first unit, and have already read *Woodsong*, encourage them to identify words from *Woodsong* that are also used in *Dogsong*. Suggest that they use these words and phrases to assist them in decoding words that pertain to Eskimo culture and experiences, such as *toggle*. If students have not yet read *Woodsong*, you might have ESL students work with an English-speaking partner to decide which terms are important to know. Then have the partners prepare to discuss at least two words with the rest of the class.

Comprehension Questions

Chapters 1–3

1 Why does Russel become angry in the morning when he hears his father coughing in the next room?

_____

2 Why does Russel's father suggest that he talk with Oogruk?

_____
_____

3 How does Oogruk explain the Eskimos' loss of their songs? Why did this happen to them?

_____
_____
_____

4 Compare Russel's relationship with his father to his relationship with Oogruk. How are they the same? In what way are they different?

_____
_____
_____
_____

Chapters 4–6

5 In what way does becoming stranded on the sea ice help Russel appreciate his dog team?

_____
_____

6 How do Russel's father and the rest of the village react when Russel tells them he is going to live with Oogruk?

_____
_____

7 Do you think Russel did the right thing, leaving Oogruk to die on the ice? Explain.

_____
_____
_____

8 Why was it important for Russel to test himself in the Arctic wilderness?

_____
_____

Comprehension Questions

Chapters 7–13

1 What is Russel's reaction to the snowmobile he finds in the wilderness? Why?

_____

2 Russel was originally going into the wilderness to find his own "song." How do you think he feels about taking a young girl along with him?

_____

_____

3 What message does *Dogsong* give the reader about the relationship between people and animals?

_____

_____

_____

Chapter 14 and Part 3

4 How did Russel's hunt turn out differently from the hunt in his dream? What does he learn from the dream?

_____

_____

_____

5 How did Nancy and Russel react to the birth of the baby? Why do you think they had this reaction?

_____

_____

6 What was Russel seeking on his journey into the wilderness? Do you think he found it? Explain your answer.

_____

_____

_____

7 What do you think Russel means when he says of his dogs, "They are me"?

_____

_____

_____

Name .... Date ....

Exploring Theme

To figure out the theme of a story, ask yourself: "What is the big idea that the story presents? What message is the author trying to send me, and what does he want me to notice?" In *Dogsong*, Russel learns a lesson about life. The lesson he learns is the theme of the story. Answer the questions below. They will help you figure out the theme of *Dogsong*.

1 How does Russel feel about Eskimo life and culture at the beginning of the book?

_____

_____

_____

2 How does Russel feel on his first outings with the dogs under Oogruk's guidance?

_____

_____

_____

3 What does Russel learn about himself from the dreams he has while running?

_____

_____

_____

4 Suppose Russel had decided not to follow Oogruk's advice, and had traveled north into the wilderness? What incorrect ideas would he have about himself and Eskimo culture?

_____

_____

_____

Choose the statement that best reflects the theme for this story. Fill in the bubble next to the answer.

○ Always listen to the advice of your elders.

○ Anyone can learn how to run a dog team if he or she practices and keeps at it.

○ It isn't the destination that counts, it's what you learn on the journey.

Exploring Character

The main character in a story has special traits, or qualities, that are usually lasting. They do not change from day to day, the way a person's feelings do. Select one character trait that describes Russel Suskitt, and add it to the character web below. Then complete the web by listing Russel's thoughts, feelings, actions, and words that illustrate this character trait.

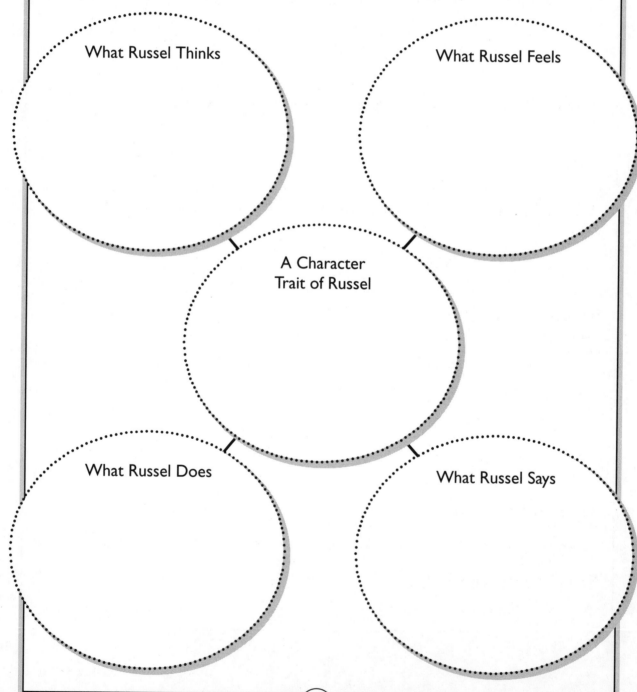

What Russel Thinks

What Russel Feels

A Character Trait of Russel

What Russel Does

What Russel Says

UNIT ONE

Writing Activities

Choose from among the following writing activities to inspire connections to *Dogsong*, as well as your students' imaginations.

Detailed Description

In *Dogsong*, Gary Paulsen uses vivid descriptions and sensory details to describe the setting. Read aloud two example paragraphs from Chapter 6:

> It was hard to believe the beauty of that torn and forlorn place. The small mountains—large hills, really—were sculpted by the wind in shapes of rounded softness, and the light...

> The light was a soft blue-purple during the day, a gentle color that goes into the eyes and becomes part of the mind and goes still deeper and deeper to enter the soul. Soul color is the daylight.

Have students write a paragraph describing a sight or setting in their neighborhood, or one experienced on a vacation. Ask students to use sensory details to make the setting come alive for the reader.

Animal Song

Invite a volunteer to read Part 3 of *Dogsong* aloud to the class. Discuss with students what the dogs mean to Russel in the song, and why they are so important to him. Then have students write their own songs about an animal that has been important to them in some way. It might be a favorite pet, or an animal they saw in a zoo or in a wilderness setting. Encourage students to emulate Paulsen's spare writing style in their "song," and provide time for volunteers to read their finished work to the class.

Journal Entry

Remind students that Russel has many conflicting feelings when he leaves Oogruk on the ice. He gets on his sled and lets the dogs run without looking back, but then he calls the team around and goes to find the old man. When Russel sees that Oogruk has died, "a place in him wanted to smile, and another place wanted to cry." Have students write a journal entry from Russel's point of view, describing his thoughts after he leaves Oogruk and begins his run north.

How-To Manual

Recall with students that Russel has to learn many things—both on his own and from Oogruk—before he can survive by himself in the Arctic wilderness. Suggest that students use information in *Dogsong* and in various reference sources to write a how-to manual about surviving in the Arctic, from Russel's point of view. Students should include what Russel learned about obtaining food, running the dogs, and surviving the cold.

UNIT ONE

Group and Individual
Classroom Projects

Choose from among the following cross-curricular activities to enhance your students' understanding of the literature selections.

Science

Paulsen discusses the difference between sea ice and freshwater ice in *Dogsong*. Using sea salt and two baking pans filled with approximately one inch of water, have students discover the difference for themselves. Have students add three tablespoons of sea salt to one of the baking pans, stirring until it is completely dissolved. Place the pans in a freezer overnight. The next day, students can examine the ice for differences.

Social Studies

Invite students to work in small groups to research the cultural history of the Inuit peoples of the Arctic Circle. Each group can concentrate on a different aspect such as food, shelter, transportation, clothing, and religious beliefs. Explain to students that with the construction of the Alaskan oil pipeline in the 1970s, the customs of many Inuit peoples changed drastically due to oil revenues and a rise in their standard of living. While enabled to purchase many modern conveniences for the first time, they also began to lose part of their ancient culture. Students can explore how the Inuit are trying to preserve their culture in an increasingly technological world. An excellent resource for students to use is *http://arcticcircle.uconn.edu/HistoryCulture*.

Art

Invite students to make a poster for a film version of *Dogsong*. Provide paper, pencils, markers, paints, and brushes. Have them scan the book to find an appealing scene. Encourage them to make a rough sketch of their poster. They can rename the movie, if they wish, and can write a sentence that promotes the film.

Science

Remind students that Russel gets lost on a run with the dogs and relies on them to find the way home. With a compass, he would have been able to figure out in which direction he was traveling. To make a compass, provide students with sponge or plastic foam, a bar magnet, needle, scissors, and a bowl of water (with a drop of detergent added to reduce surface tension). Be sure students are careful handling the needle. Have them rub the needle—in one direction only—against one end of the magnet for one minute. Then have them push the magnetized needle through the center of a small piece of sponge until it protrudes equally on both sides. Then place the sponge in the water so that it floats and the needle is parallel to the water. Have students compare the direction in which their needles point; and hypothesize how their compasses work.

Unit Discussion Questions

1. What words would you use to describe Gary Paulsen in *Woodsong*? What words would you use to describe Russel Suskitt? In what way are the two characters similar?

2. Both *Woodsong* and *Dogsong* contain the word *song* in their titles. What is the "song of the woods" as Paulsen sees it in *Woodsong*? What is the "song of the dogs" in *Dogsong*? How are these two songs similar?

3. In Part Three of *Dogsong*, Paulsen writes:

   Come, see my dogs.

   > My dogs are what lead me,
   > they are what move me.
   > See my dogs in the steam,
   > in the steam of my life.
   > They are me.

   In what way do these words relate to both Gary Paulsen in *Woodsong* and Russel in *Dogsong*?

4. Both Gary Paulsen and Russel have "lessons in blood" that affect them and change their lives in some way. In what way are these lessons similar in both *Woodsong* and *Dogsong*? How are they different?

5. What role do animals play in both *Woodsong* and *Dogsong*? What lessons do these animals teach the main characters in each book?

6. Imagine a conversation between Russel and Gary Paulsen. What do you think they would have to say to each other if they met somewhere on the Alaskan tundra?

7. As Russel and his dog team travel north into the remote Alaskan interior, they master the intricacies of wilderness survival—overcoming the hardships of hunger and fear. It is here that Russel comes face to face with his vision of Russel the mammoth hunter, a part-real, part-mythic ancestor of another time, and another dimension of Russel's undiscovered self. Near the beginning of Chapter 14, Paulsen writes of Russel:

   > The dream had folded into his life and his life had folded back into the dream so many times that it was not possible for him to find which was real and which was dream.

   How is Russel's dream similar to the hallucinations that Paulsen experiences on the Iditarod? In what way is it different?

Hatchet

Synopsis

Hatchet is perhaps the most popular of Paulsen's novels, a Newbery Honor Book in 1988. In the opening pages, 13-year-old Brian Robeson, still reeling from his parents' sudden divorce, is on his way to visit his father in Canada. Brian is on board a small Cessna 406 with a pilot of few words, a man who, Brian feels, "seems more like a machine than a human being." About an hour into the flight, the pilot complains of chest pains, and Brian quickly realizes the man is having a heart attack. Brian frantically, but unsuccessfully, radios for help. When the plane runs out of fuel he manages to crash-land in a wilderness lake. The pilot has died at the controls, but Brian, after nearly drowning in the cold water, is able to pull himself out of the lake. Crawling ashore, he soon falls asleep underneath the branches of a tall pine tree.

Upon awakening, Brian takes stock of his situation. He knows that the plane has gone off-course, and it may take a while before a rescue party can find him. He has managed to salvage his hatchet, a parting gift from his mother, but otherwise, the only asset he has is himself. He finds shelter and some berries to eat, but when a porcupine invades a cave he has found during his first night in the wilderness and shoots quills into his leg, Brian suddenly becomes overwhelmed by his situation and begins to cry. When he pulls himself together, he realizes he has learned "the most important rule of survival—feeling sorry for yourself [doesn't] work."

The next morning, Brian remembers the shower of sparks that flew from the cave wall when he threw the hatchet at the porcupine in an attempt to scare it away. He uses stones from the cave, his hatchet, and some kindling to make a fire before the end of his second day. Over the next several weeks, Brian labors diligently to set up a camp, gathering wood, and teaching himself new skills, such as fishing without a rod and reel. He despairs for a moment when a rescue plane flies over the area and doesn't see him, but the changes that have gradually taken place in Brian since the plane crash—both mentally and physically—have given him the knowledge and confidence he needs to carry on.

This confidence also helps Brian to deal with a number of setbacks: An angry moose heaves Brian into the lake at one point, hurting him badly, and a fierce wind storm one evening nearly destroys his shelter. But the storm also accomplishes something else: It brings the downed plane to the surface of the lake, and Brian decides to make an attempt to retrieve the survival bag he knows is still on board. It's a difficult undertaking, and the sight of the dead pilot is traumatic, but he succeeds. As Brian is eating his first meal made from the contents of the bag, a plane lands and rescues him.

Setting a Purpose for Reading

Invite students to skim the book and to read the synopsis on the inside dust jacket or on the back of the book. Students might then wish to set their own purposes for reading, or you can prompt discussion with the following questions:

1 Why do you suppose Gary Paulsen decided to call this story *Hatchet*? Why would a hatchet be a valuable tool to have in the wilderness?

2 What kinds of problems do you think Brian will have to overcome before he can find his way back to civilization?

3 What lessons will Brian learn from the wilderness as he struggles to survive? How will these be similar to and different from the lessons Gary Paulsen learned in the woods in *Woodsong*, and the lessons Russel Suskitt learned on the ice in *Dogsong*?

Literary Element: Plot

Point out to students that recognizing a character's problems and how he or she solves those problems helps the reader discover a story's structure or basic plan, follow the story line, identify the plot, and understand the story as a whole. It also makes it possible to understand why characters act in certain ways and how they change. Define the following terms for students by writing them on the chalkboard and having a volunteer read them aloud. Then have students use a chart like the one below to record some of the problems Brian Robeson faces, and their eventual solution.

❋ problem: what a main character wants to do, wants to find out, or wants to change about a situation that he or she is in

❋ turning point: the point at which the character experiences a big change—when the problem ends and the solution begins

❋ solution: an action or decision that makes it clear to the character how to achieve what he or she wants to do

Problem	Turning Point	Solution

Literary Element: Mood

Explain to students that mood is the feeling or atmosphere an author creates in a story. Authors use mood to give a story a particular feeling and to evoke certain emotions in the reader. They carefully select words and compose sentences with descriptive details to create a certain atmosphere. Point out that there can be as many moods in the story as there are feelings. Sometimes there is a shift in story mood to show how the feelings of the characters have changed. Write the following chart on the board as an example. Students can use it to track Brian's changing moods as he learns to survive in the wilderness.

Event/Setting	Descriptive Words	Mood
Canadian north woods after the crash	Felt the hair on the back of his neck go up Things might be looking at him right now	Fear

Vocabulary

Have students create a word web built around the concept of wilderness survival. Ask students to add categories such as *food*, *shelter*, and *animals*. As students read the book, have them add words to each category, such as *aspens*, *spruce*, *hummocks*, *berries*, *skunk*, and *porcupine*. When students have finished reading, they can share what they know as well as the context clues they used to decode each word.

ESL As they read *Hatchet*, students will encounter the names of various parts of an airplane that may be unfamiliar to them, such as *vertical stabilizer*, *fuselage*, and *cargo hatch*. If possible, you may want to show ESL students pictures of these plane parts to help them define the words. The following words from the book are difficult to decode using context clues. You may wish to define these terms for students:

ruefully with a feeling of pity

eddy a circular current of air or water

self-pity a state of feeling sorry for oneself

substantial important; having significance

eeled swam in an elusive or slippery way

coupled in addition to

UNIT TWO

Comprehension Questions

Chapters 1–4

1 Why is Brian so upset at the beginning of the novel?

_____

_____

2 What is "The Secret," or the memory Brian wakes up to after the crash?

_____

3 What noises does Brian discover in the wilderness? How are they different from the noises that surround him at home?

_____

_____

4 In what way is Brian's situation different from that faced by Gary Paulsen in *Woodsong* or by Russel in *Dogsong*?

_____

_____

_____

Chapters 5–8

5 Why is Brian shocked by what follows after he shouts, "I'm hungry!"?

_____

_____

6 What are all the assets Brian lists when he begins to think about survival? Which do you think is the most important? Why?

_____

_____

_____

7 When Brian is eating raspberries, what does he learn from his encounter with a bear?

_____

_____

8 What does Brian discover he must have in order to survive?

_____

_____

UNIT
TWO

Comprehension Questions

Chapters 9–12

1. How do fire and the discovery of the turtle eggs begin to change Brian's thinking about survival?

_____

_____

2. What does Brian learn from the kingfisher? How does this compare to what Gary Paulsen learns from the animals in *Woodsong*?

_____

_____

3. Why does Brian momentarily give up hope when he sees the search plane?

_____

_____

Chapter 13–Epilogue

4. How does Brian's encounter with the wolf demonstrate how he has changed since the first days after the crash?

_____

_____

5. How does Brian's new method of looking for foolbirds in the forest change his life in the woods?

_____

_____

6. Why is Brian's temporary loss of the hatchet more significant than the other problems he has faced since the crash?

_____

_____

_____

7. How has Brian changed at the end of the book?

_____

_____

_____

Name .... Date ....

HATCHET

UNIT TWO

Exploring Plot

To help you follow the storyline and identify the plot of *Hatchet*, complete the chart below by filling in the appropriate problem or solution from the story.

Problem	Solution
"I'm hungry." He said it aloud. In normal tones at first, then louder and louder until he was yelling it. "I'm hungry, I'm hungry, I'm hungry!"	
	He set about improving his shelter by tearing it down. From dead pines up the hill he brought down heavier logs and fastened several of them across the opening, wedging them at the top and burying the bottoms in the sand. It all held together like a very stiff woven basket.
The fish spear didn't work. He stood in the shallows and waited, again and again. The small fish came closer and closer and he lunged time after time but was always too slow. He tried throwing it, jabbing it, everything but flailing with it, and it didn't work. The fish were just too fast.	
	Soon, under an hour, there were thirty or forty small fish in the enclosure and Brian made a gate by weaving small willows together into a fine mesh and closed them in.
If I could get at the pack, he thought. It probably had food and knives and matches. It might have a sleeping bag. If I could get at the pack and just get some of those things. I would be rich. So rich if I could get at the pack.	

HATCHET

Exploring Mood

Read the two passages below from *Hatchet*. Identify the feeling that each passage evokes. Then add more details about the character and setting that enhance or add to that feeling.

> Too much. Too much. His mind screamed in horror and he slammed back and was sick in the water, sick so that he choked on it and tried to breathe water and could have ended there, ended with the pilot where it almost ended when they first arrived except that his legs jerked. It was instinctive, fear more than anything else, fear of what he had seen. But they jerked and pushed and he was headed up when they jerked and he shot to the surface, still inside the birdcage of formers and cables.

1 **What is the mood or feeling of this passage?**

_____

_____

2 **What are additional details that convey that idea?**

_____

_____

_____

_____

> I can't take it this way, alone with no fire and in the dark, and next time it might be something worse, maybe a bear, and it wouldn't be just quills in the leg, it would be worse. I can't do this, he thought, again and again. I can't. Brian pulled himself up until he was sitting upright back in the corner of the cave. He put his head down on his arms across his knees, with stiffness taking his left leg, and cried until he was cried out.

3 **What is the mood or feeling of this passage?**

_____

_____

4 **What are additional details that convey that idea?**

_____

_____

_____

_____

Writing Activities

Choose from among the following writing activities to inspire connections to *Hatchet*, as well as your students' imaginations.

Exploring Foreshadowing

Point out to students how Gary Paulsen uses foreshadowing, or a hint of what is to come, to build suspense in *Hatchet*. Read the following passage from Chapter 8 and then discuss it with students:

> . . . In the still darkness of the shelter in the middle of the night his eyes came open and he was awake and he thought there was a growl. But it was the wind, a medium wind in the pines had made some sound that brought him up, brought him awake. He sat up and was hit with the smell. It terrified him . . .

Have students write a new scene for the novel in which Brian confronts something that frightens him. Instruct students to use foreshadowing to help build suspense about a dangerous event that may or may not happen.

Journal Entry

Invite students to reread passages in *Hatchet* that describe Brian's feelings about surviving in the wilderness. You might wish to break up the class into small groups to brainstorm some strong adjectives and verbs that might help them describe Brian's feelings. Then, individually, have students imagine that Brian found paper and pencil in the survival kit. Ask them each to write a journal entry from Brian's point of view. Encourage them to use the language and ideas they've learned from reading the account of Brian's survival.

News Article

Remind students that after his rescue, the press made much of Brian and he was interviewed several times. Have students write a news article about Brian that might have appeared in their local paper. Remind them to write a headline for their article, and to answer the questions *who*, *what*, *where*, *when*, *why*, and *how*.

Exploring Point of View

While Brian encounters many animals in the woods, we see everything in the story from his point of view. Suggest that students try rewriting one of Brian's confrontations with one of the animals in *Hatchet* from the animal's point of view. How would the bear feel, for example, when it sees Brian? Why would it decide not to attack him?

Group and Individual

Classroom Projects

Choose from among the following cross-curricular activities to enhance your students' understanding of the literature selections.

Science

When Brian returns home, he researches some of the animals he encountered while in the wilderness. Have students conduct additional research on Canada and list some other animals Brian might have encountered. For example, are coyotes or mountain lions found in this area of Canada? Students can present their findings to the class, including pictures of the animals and information about their characteristics. Students can also discuss whether Brian would have to be cautious around these animals.

Art

Hatchet is filled with images of fast-paced action. Students who are artistically inclined might enjoy illustrating these scenes for a graphic version of the story. Suggest that they divide the scene into a series of events—including a beginning, middle, and end. The events in each part should be listed, as well as illustrated. Students might wish to work in groups on this project, putting their scenes together in the correct sequence to display a complete story.

Geography

Using maps, students can compare the United States with Canada. You will need to distribute both physical and political maps of North America. Working with partners, students can find the areas of the United States that might be similar to the one in Canada where Brian was stranded. To distinguish settled areas from wilderness areas, partners can look at the geographical features of the two countries, as well as the locations of cities, railroads, and roads. If necessary, help students understand the symbols used on each map. Partners can take notes and present their ideas to the class, explaining the map clues they used.

Math

Based on information found in *Hatchet*, students can determine the length of Brian's plane. First, to make a scale drawing of the Canadian lake where the plane crashed, students can approximate the depth of the lake from the information about Brian's dive in Chapter 18. Then they can estimate the plane's angle in the water based on the information in Chapter 17. Students can then choose a scale and draw a triangle with the base representing the lake bottom and the hypotenuse representing the plane. Have students use their diagrams to estimate the length of the plane. Remind them to add the length of the tail assembly above the water to the plane's overall length.

The River

Synopsis

In this first sequel to *Hatchet*, 15-year-old Brian Robeson is back in New York, living with his mother, and happy that the media attention surrounding his experience in the Canadian wilderness has finally subsided. Yet he remains forever changed by his ordeal. He cannot walk through a city park without watching the trees for game. And after months of trapping and looking for food, a grocery store is still a miracle.

Then one day three government officials arrive on Brian's doorstep and propose that he return to the wilderness so that NASA and the military can learn and record the survival techniques Brian discovered to keep himself alive. Initially, both Brian and his mother dismiss the idea as insane, but when Brian realizes that what he learned might help others to survive, he agrees to return to Canada.

This time, however, Brian won't be alone. He will be accompanied by Derek Holtzer, a government psychologist who will take notes and record everything that happens. However, when Brian sees all the survival gear Holtzer plans to bring with them—including a rifle, an inflatable raft, and food rations—he refuses to embark from the plane unless Holtzer leaves it all behind. "You want to learn," Brian says, "but if you have all that backup, it's just more games. It's not real. You wouldn't have that if the situation were real, would you?" Finally, Brian accepts a compromise. He allows Holtzer to bring a radio along so they can wire for help if it's absolutely necessary.

On their first night, Brian and Derek battle swarms of hungry mosquitoes. But soon Brian finds a fire stone, and before long they are able to gather and trap sufficient food. They eventually settle into what becomes, for Brian, more of a camping trip than a survival experience. He begins to wish they would have some trouble that would make the whole experience more realistic.

Soon enough, his wish is granted. When a freak lightning storm knocks out the radio transmitter and leaves Derek in a coma, Brian finds his survival skills are put to the ultimate test: Now he is not only responsible for himself but for the life of another person as well. Fearing that Derek will die of dehydration before anyone notices their radio is out, Brian realizes that his only option is to build a makeshift raft and try to get Derek 100 miles downriver where he will find a trading post, according to Derek's map. Battling rapids, exhaustion, and his own hallucinations and demons, Brian finally reaches safety and emerges from this new experience with a friend and some new truths about himself.

Setting a Purpose for Reading

The River is a sequel to Gary Paulsen's *Hatchet*. You may wish to have a classroom discussion about what Brian Robeson learned during his first experience in the wilderness and how this knowledge might help him when he returns. Then encourage students to read the back cover or dust jacket of the book. Use the following questions to stimulate additional discussion and help students set a purpose for reading:

1 Why would Brian decide to return to the wilderness after his harrowing experience in *Hatchet*?

2 What life-threatening situations might Brian encounter in this new adventure? How might what he learned during his first experience in the wilderness help him to survive here?

3 In *The River*, Brian returns to Canada accompanied by a government psychologist. How might having a companion make this trip easier for Brian? In what ways might it be more difficult?

Comprehension Strategy: Summary

When your students are able to summarize, it indicates to you that they understand a variety of literary elements—especially character, setting, and plot. Explain to students that being able to summarize helps them to better understand the story as a whole.

Remind students that plot is comprised of several important related events or actions, including the problem, the turning points or events that lead to solving the problem, and the solution to the problem. Turning points, where the action can go in a variety of directions, create tension and suspense for the reader, who wants to find out how the problem will be resolved.

Point out that the important events that make up a plot may not always be presented in a progressive sequence. An author may go back in time to tell about something that has a strong bearing on the present situation. Discuss the use of this narrative technique, known as flashback, and how Gary Paulsen utilized it in *Hatchet*. Ask students how Paulsen might use flashbacks in *The River*, when Brian returns to the wilderness.

As students read, remind them to be alert to the sequence of events in the story and to any cause-and-effect relationships that result. Identifying these relationships can help them pinpoint the problem or problems the major character faces at different times in the story, and how they are resolved.

The reproducible on page 44 will help your students to better understand how to summarize by providing them with a framework for identifying the important points to include in a summary.

Literary Element: Author's Language

Instruction in appreciating author's language will help students recognize certain words and sounds authors use to enhance their stories. Write the following literary devices and their definitions on the board, and ask volunteers to think of examples of each.

✳ alliteration: repetition of beginning sounds in neighboring words; often used to add a pleasing, melodic sound or to evoke in readers' minds specific sounds

✳ onomatopoeia: words that imitate the sounds made by something (*swish*, *clang*)

✳ sensory words: words that appeal to the senses (flies *buzzed*/sound, fire *glowed*/sight)

✳ personification: lifelike qualities attributed to an inanimate object, such as a rock

✳ simile: comparison of two things using the word *like* or *as*

✳ metaphor: comparison of two things without using the words *like* or *as*

✳ idiom: expression that cannot be understood from the literal meaning of its words

Have students look for each of these devices as they read *The River*.

Vocabulary

The River contains specialized vocabulary that relates to aviation. Write the following terms on the chalkboard: *flaps*, *taxied*, *descent*, *rudder pedals*, *altitude*, *bush plane*, *throttle*, *runway*, *amphibious float*, *propeller*, *banked*, and *throttling*. Have students arrange the words into a web around the word *aviation*, and the categories "Parts of a Plane" and "Words That Describe a Plane's Motion." As they read, students can use context clues to find the meaning of unfamiliar words. Then, students can keep track of new words they've learned by placing them on a chart like the one below:

VOCABULARY

Aviation Term	Meaning

ESL ▾ *The River*, like almost all books in English, contains many multiple-meaning words that may present problems for students whose first language is not English. Write the following words and their definitions on the board. Have students look for them as they read and use context clues to figure out which definition is used in the book.

bark covering on the outside of a tree   to speak angrily

pose to hold a certain position   to present something

bolt discharge of lightning   to leave suddenly

pupil opening in center of eye   student

buckled fastened   collapsed

bank to cover a fire so it will burn slowly   place where money is kept

Comprehension Questions

Chapters 1–6

1 Who are the three men who visit Brian? Why do they want him to return to the wilderness?

_____

_____

2 In what ways has Brian changed as a result of his experience in the wilderness?

_____

_____

3 Why does Brian insist that Derek leave all the cargo he has brought on the plane?

_____

_____

4 How does Brian instantly change when he steps off the plane and into the wilderness?

_____

_____

_____

Chapters 7–12

5 Brian knows from his first experience that luck played an important part in his survival, and that good luck often followed bad luck. What bad luck do Brian and Derek experience? How does it lead to good luck?

_____

_____

_____

6 Why does Brian reach the conclusion that survival cannot be taught and that the experiment wasn't working?

_____

_____

7 What happens to both Brian and Derek during the storm?

_____

_____

8 What memory does Derek's condition awaken in Brian?

_____

UNIT
TWO

Comprehension Questions

Chapters 13–18

1 Why does Brian reach the conclusion that he cannot leave Derek behind when he goes to seek help?

_____

_____

2 What strategy does Brian develop to maneuver the raft along the river?

_____

_____

_____

3 Why does Brian hallucinate his first night on the raft? What kind of hallucinations does he experience?

_____

_____

_____

Chapters 19–24

4 In what way is the waterfall Brian hears a turning point in the plot?

_____

_____

_____

5 What happens to both Brian and Derek when the raft hits a submerged rock in the river?

_____

_____

6 How are Brian and Derek finally rescued?

_____

_____

7 What happens to Derek after the rescue?

_____

_____

8 How has his experience on the river changed Brian?

_____

_____

Name .... Date ....

UNIT TWO

GRAPHIC ORGANIZER

Exploring Summary

To help you summarize, fill in the boxes below by adding key information from the story.

Title/Author	Characters	Setting

Problem	Events/Turning Points	Solution

Using the information you have organized in boxes above, write a paragraph that summarizes the story:

____

____

____

____

____

____

What do you think is the author's purpose in writing this book?

____

____

____

Exploring Author's Language

Read the passages below from *The River*. Underline the literary device in each passage.
Then fill in the blank with the correct literary device to label each passage.

> metaphor   alliteration   simile   idiom
> sensory words   onomatopoeia   personification

1

_____

The mud was so thick it pulled his right tennis shoe off, and when he groped to find it the mud held his arm, seemed to pull at him, tried to take him down.

2

_____

The mosquitoes. Tearing at him, clouds of them, the awful, ripping, thick masses of the small monsters trying to bleed him dry.

3

_____

Like a camera taking pictures with a strobe light, things would seem frozen in time.

4

_____

He met a girl in school, Deborah McKenzie. They hit it off and went on a few dates.

5

_____

. . . curling up into his eyes there came the tiny flicker of new flame.

6

_____

. . . see nothing but images frozen in the split instants of brilliance from the lightning.

7

_____

But there it was again. A hissing? Was that it?
No.
It was lower than that. Not to be heard, but felt.
A *whooshing* — water.
A water sound.

UNIT TWO

Writing Activities

Choose from among the following writing activities to inspire connections to *The River*, as well as your students' imaginations.

Journal Entry

Recall with students that, initially, Derek's idea of what will happen in the wilderness is very different from Brian's. Although Derek has been on survival training trips, he has always carried a minimum amount of gear with him to smooth the way. He is shocked, then, when Brian tells him to leave all his equipment on the plane: "If you have all that backup, it's just more games," Brian says. "It's not real." Have students write a journal entry that Derek might have written after his first day in the wilderness with Brian. What would Derek write about his experiences so far? What might he expect to encounter in the days to come?

New Dialogue

Point out to students that authors often advance the plots of their stories through dialogue. Have students reread the last page of *The River*, where Brian's mother and father vow never to let him go into the woods again and Brian argues that, of all people who were qualified to be in the wilderness, he was certainly one of them. Have students rewrite this scene, imagining the dialogue that might have transpired between Brian and his parents. What examples of his expertise might Brian have given his parents? What arguments might Brian's parents have used?

Alternate Scene

Discuss with students how Brian's previous experience in the wilderness proved to be of great benefit in getting both Brian and Derek to safety. Ask students to imagine what might have happened if Brian had been struck by lightning and had fallen into a coma. What would Derek have done if the radio transmitter failed to work? Have students review the chapter in which Brian discovers Derek's situation and then rewrite it, imagining what Derek would have done in a similar situation.

Exploring Literary Device

Review with students the literary devices of alliteration, onomatopoeia, metaphor, simile, personification, idiom, and sensory words. Suggest that interested students look through *The River* for additional examples of each of these devices. Then, using the same plot and characters from *The River*, have them write sentences that include their own example of each device.

Group and Individual
Classroom Projects

Choose from among the following cross-curricular activities to enhance your students' understanding of the literature selections.

Art

Although *The River* is not illustrated, Paulsen provides many descriptions of the scenery surrounding Brian and Derek. Read aloud with students the paragraph in Chapter 12 that begins "It was full light now..." Discuss the view that Brian sees before him from the shelter. Then have students look through the book for other descriptions of the wilderness that they can use to illustrate a scene from *The River*. Supply students with paper, colored markers and pens, tempera paints, and watercolors.

Language Arts

Suggest that students work in small groups to create a radio play of *The River*. Remind them that a radio play consists only of background music, sound effects, and actors' voices. Have students choose a scene to dramatize and a narrator to give appropriate background information. Small groups can work to find suitable sound effects and background music for the scene. Provide students with rehearsal space. They can then present their scenes to the class.

Math

Recall with students that after Derek falls into a coma, Brian must calculate how long it will take him to get to Bannock's Trading Post. Looking at the map Derek has brought with him, Brian notes that it is laid out in grids and that each grid represents five kilometers. Brian slowly counts out 150 kilometers on the map and deduces that the trading post is 100 miles away, given that there are 1.6 kilometers to a mile. Suggest that a group of students use this information from the map to create math exercises. When they have finished, they can exchange papers and try to solve each other's problems.

Science

Remind students that swarms of biting mosquitoes attack Brian and Derek on their first night in the wilderness. About a week later, during a violent storm, a lightning bolt short-circuits Derek's radio and sends him into a coma. Working in two groups, have students research both mosquitoes and lightning. Ask these questions to get them started: What is the lifecycle of a mosquito? Where are they found? Why are they dangerous to humans? What is lightning? How can it short-circuit a radio or send someone into a coma? Each group can make charts that list interesting facts and safety tips about their topic, and report their findings to the rest of the class.

Brian's Winter

Synopsis

Brian's Winter was published in 1996, eight years after *Hatchet*. It was written, in Gary Paulsen's words, "for all those readers (I received as many as two hundred letters a day) who wrote to tell me they felt Brian Robeson's story was left unfinished by the early rescue—before, they said, 'it became really hard going.'" Paulsen himself had faced many brutal winters in northern Minnesota, and the challenge interested him. The result was a book detailing what could and perhaps would have happened to Brian had he not been rescued after 42 days in the wilderness.

As Paulsen notes in the foreword to *Brian's Winter*, for the purposes of this book, it is necessary to shift the idea left by *Hatchet* and suppose that although Brian did retrieve the survival pack from the plane, he did not trigger a radio signal and was not rescued. Yet the book stands alone and can be read independently of its predecessor.

Fall comes on with a softness in *Brian's Winter*, so soft that Brian doesn't realize what he is in for until it is almost too late. Out hunting one day, he feels a new coolness, a touch on his cheek like a soft kiss. Brian's winter survival is chronicled in great detail as he slowly learns how to navigate through the woods after a blizzard, and make the clothes he needs to help him stay warm in subzero temperatures. An uneasy alliance is struck with a hungry skunk that turns out to be an unexpected ally when a voracious bear invades Brian's camp searching for food. Through it all, Brian relies on his instincts and his intelligence to confront the deadliest enemy he has yet faced: a "hard-spined north woods winter." And he learns that the surest way to survive is to never rest and never grow complacent. Nature is always working.

Brian is finally rescued when he comes across a Cree trapping family, the Smallhorns, not far from his own camp. The supply plane that brings them provisions every six weeks finally takes Brian back home. As Brian leaves, David Smallhorn touches him on the shoulder and waves an arm around at the woods and lake and sky. "It will all be here when you get back," he says.

Setting a Purpose for Reading

Before students read the book, discuss the topic of winter and the seasons. Elicit from students some of the beauties of winter, but make sure they understand some of the dangers of extreme cold as well. Having read *Hatchet*, ask students what additional dangers they think Brian might face in the sequel *Brian's Winter*. Encourage students to make a KWL chart like the one shown on page 49, which they can add to as they read the book.

What I Know	What I Want to Know	What I Learned

Comprehension Strategy: Sequence

Explain to students that recognizing and understanding time-order relationships in *Brian's Winter* will enable them to track the sequence of events in the book. It will also help them understand the motivations of the main character as well as cause-and-effect situations that arise in the development of the plot. Point out that these time-order relationships may be explicitly stated by the author's use of signal words, or they may need to be inferred by the reader. The time order in which events occur may also be presented in a reversed sequence or simultaneously.

In addition, explain to students that a flashback is an interruption in the chronological flow of a narrative to a time in the past. A flashforward is an interruption in the sequence of events to a time in the future. As students read, ask them to pay particular attention to the following points to help them recognize the sequence of events in the book:

* Signal words are words that an author uses to give clues to the sequence of events in a story. Tell students that they should be alert to words such as *first, second, third, then, before, after, into, last, since, later, next, now, while, until, during, always, one time,* and *earlier* as they read to help them recognize the sequence of events.

* Authors sometimes omit events in a chronological sequence, especially if the sequence involves the kind of action that the reader has experienced before with the same character. Suggest that students remain alert to clues that might suggest an event omitted from a sequence.

Literary Element: Tone

Explain to students that the tone of a book is the author's attitude or feeling toward the characters, events, or information in his or her written work, and that tone is an author's manner of "speaking." Authors express emotions through tone, and readers must infer an author's tone through the printed word rather than the sound of a voice. In order for readers to know the tone of the story, an author must use words that consistently reveal his or her attitude or feeling toward the characters and events he or she creates.

Point out to students that it is easy to confuse tone with mood or atmosphere. Remind them that mood refers to a book's overall emotion or feeling—suspense, optimism, cheerfulness. Explain to students that when they are trying to determine the tone of a story, they have to look for the author's attitude toward characters, events, or information.

Vocabulary

Explain to students that many of the vocabulary words they encountered in *Hatchet* will reappear in *Brian's Winter*. Point out, however, that winter weather will bring Brian a host of new problems that he did not have to deal with in *Hatchet*, and he will need to make a number of new tools and clothing accessories to help him through the cold temperatures. Write the words *arrowhead, hardwood, tipi, enclosure, hide, deerskin, snowshoe, windbreaker, bow, lance, spear,* and *rawhide* on the chalkboard. Create a chart with the headings "Shelter," "Apparel," and "Weapons," and then ask students to list the words under the appropriate heading. Suggest that they look for context clues as they read to define words with which they are unfamiliar.

ESL *Arrowhead, hardwood, deerskin, snowshoe, windbreaker,* and *rawhide,* from the list of words written on the chalkboard, are examples of compound words found in *Brian's Winter* that can be decoded from their two base words. You may wish to point out to second-language learners that while the compound words provided as an example are closed, others can be open or hyphenated. Invite students to list the compound words from the chalkboard and write a brief definition for each, based on the meanings of the individual words that make up the compound. They can add to their list of compound words as they read *Brian's Winter*.

**UNIT
TWO**

Comprehension Questions

Chapters 1–4

1 Why does Brian become so angry after he eats all of the freeze-dried food from the survival kit?

_____

_____

2 In what way is Brian his own worst enemy in these early chapters of the book?

_____

_____

3 How do the rain and the migrating geese serve as a warning to Brian that winter is coming?

_____

_____

4 How does Brian feel when he hears the wolves just before falling asleep? How is this feeling different from the way he might have felt just after the crash?

_____

_____

_____

_____

Chapters 5–8

5 What happens as a result of the wolf kill Brian stumbles upon?

_____

_____

6 Why does Brian suddenly decide to go hunting for deer?

_____

_____

7 In what way does Betty turn out to be a true friend to Brian?

_____

8 How is the first snow Brian experiences in the woods different from the snowfalls he has seen in the city and park where he lives?

_____

9 What makes Brian decide that the snow will make hunting easier for him?

_____

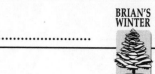

UNIT TWO

Comprehension Questions

....

Chapters 9–11

1 Why does Brian feel both good and bad after a successful hunt?

_____

2 Why does Betty stop visiting Brian for her daily feedings?

_____

Chapters 12–14

3 Where does Brian first get the idea to make snowshoes?

_____

4 Why do you think Brian considers the hatchet his mother made him take along on the trip the key to his survival?

_____

_____

5 Why does Brian think he hears gunshots in the middle of the night? What is it that he actually hears?

_____

_____

6 In what way do the snowshoes change the way that Brian feels about winter?

_____

_____

Chapter 15–Epilogue

7 Why does Brian become so upset when he watches the wolf pack hunt and kill the moose?

_____

_____

8 What causes Brian to go in search of the popping sounds he hears one morning?

_____

9 Why does Brian have a hard time leaving the woods when the supply plane arrives to take him home?

_____

_____

BRIAN'S
WINTER

UNIT
TWO

GRAPHIC ORGANIZER

Exploring Sequence

Look at the following events from *Brian's Winter*. For each event, write an event from the story that came before it and one that came after it.

1

BEFORE	EVENT	AFTER
	A bear invades Brian's camp in the middle of the night, and Brian kicks it. →	

2

BEFORE	EVENT	AFTER
	Brian discovers that everything that moves in the woods leaves tracks in the snow. →	

3

BEFORE	EVENT	AFTER
	Brian hears a popping sound and then realizes it's too warm for trees to explode. →	

On a separate sheet of paper, write a sequence of events for what might happen to Brian when he returns home and is considered a hero for surviving so long in the wilderness on his own.

GRAPHIC ORGANIZER

Exploring Tone

Choose an event from *Brian's Winter* and think about Gary Paulsen's attitude, or feeling, about the event. Does he think it's amusing or perhaps frightening? In other words, what tone does he use to describe the event? Think about the story details and the words he chooses to describe the event and the characters. Use the graphic organizer below to record your thoughts. Then decide on the tone the author uses.

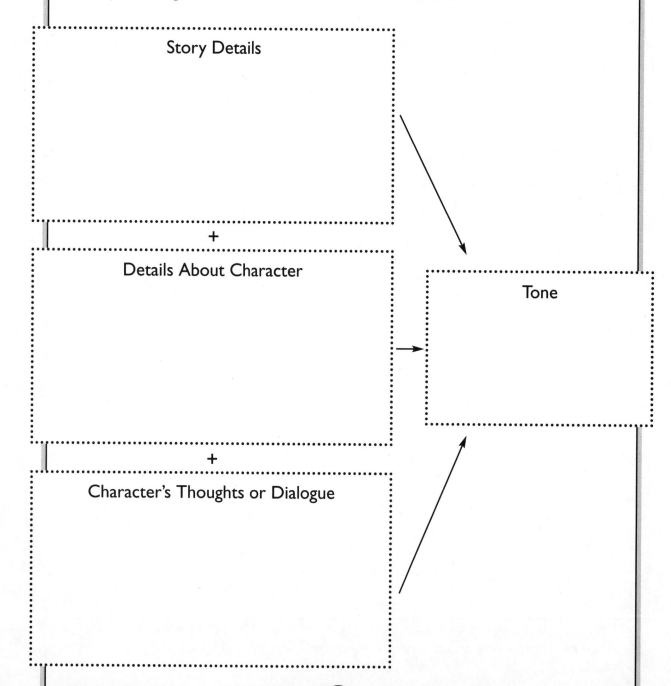

Story Details

+

Details About Character

Tone

+

Character's Thoughts or Dialogue

Writing Activities

Choose from among the following writing activities to inspire connections to *Brian's Winter*, as well as your students' imaginations.

Exploring Suspense

Have students reread the scene in Chapter 15, beginning with "Thirty-five yards. Still too far—twice too far," when Brian spots a deer and slowly begins to stalk it. Discuss how Paulsen builds suspense in this sequence, and helps the reader to feel the tension as Brian literally holds his breath, cautiously approaching the animal. Then ask students what techniques Paulsen uses to create tension in this scene. Elicit from them that he draws out the sequence with a series of short sentences to create anticipation. Suggest that students try this technique in their own writing. They can write a brief scene in which a character faces a tense situation.

Journal Entry

Discuss with students the different animals that Brian encounters in *Brian's Winter*, and his relationship with each of them. Then ask students to write a journal entry describing Brian's relationship with the skunk he names Betty, and how it differs from the other animals he meets. Suggest that students continue their journal entry by writing about one of the scenes between Brian and Betty—from the skunk's point of view. How would Betty feel about Brian? How would she feel about the bear who invades Brian's shelter? Encourage students to share their entries with the rest of the class.

A Letter

Recall with students that when Brian first meets the Smallhorn family, he is so surprised to see other people in the wilderness that he doesn't know what to say. He can't even remember the last time he had spoken to another person. Have students imagine how Brian feels when he returns home, and the adjustments he has to make. Suggest that they write a letter to the Smallhorn family—one that Brian might have written—thanking them for their kindness and including a description of his homecoming.

Survival Story

Suggest that students review Brian's situation in *Brian's Winter* and note the steps he took to survive in the woods. Then have students use some of these steps to write their own survival story. Explain to students that this story does not necessarily have to be set in the north woods of Canada but might take place on a tropical island or even the desert. Remind them to include details about the setting, characters, their problems, and how they will meet their needs in order to survive.

UNIT TWO

Group and Individual
Classroom Projects

Choose from among the following cross-curricular activities to enhance your students' understanding of the literature selections.

Art

Suggest that interested students make a diorama of Brian's campsite. Provide materials such as art supplies, cardboard, clay, scissors, tape, glue, paint, brushes, and colored construction paper. Then have students look back at the book, particularly Chapter 4, to see how Brian winterized his shelter. Instruct students to look for details in the text to determine what elements they'll use in the diorama. You may wish to have students form small groups to work on individual elements. Display the completed dioramas in the classroom.

Science

Winter is the coldest season of the year, but temperatures vary in different parts of the globe. The Northern Hemisphere has winter weather during December, January, February, and early March. In the Southern Hemisphere, winter begins in late June and lasts through September. Have students research the kind of weather Brian experienced in the Canadian north. How much does the temperature vary? How much snowfall could Brian expect? Students can record their information on a graph or chart and then report their findings to the class.

Science

Brian encounters many different animals in the woods, and he comes to understand some of their habits through simple observation. Have students work in small groups to investigate some of the animals Brian sees—timber wolves, skunks, and bears—and research their habits, the kinds of food they eat, and the shelters they seek out for sleeping and raising their young. For example, grizzly bears as well as brown and black bears can be found in the Northern Hemisphere. What kind of bear was Brian most likely to encounter in the Canadian wilderness? Students can report their findings to the class.

Social Studies

Remind students that at the end of *Brian's Winter*, Brian meets, and is ultimately rescued by, a Cree trapping family. When David Smallhorn sees Brian, he says, "How come is it you have skins for clothes and stone arrowheads? You look like one of the old-way people." Point out that Smallhorn is referring to the way the Cree used to live many years ago. Have students research the Cree, a people who live in Canada and in certain areas of Montana in the United States. Students' research can center on Cree history, customs, and the way many Cree live today in Canada. Have them record their findings and report them to the class.

Unit Discussion Questions

1. What knowledge of the woods does Brian bring to his experience with Derek Holtzer in *The River*? How does this affect their relationship, and why is Brian's silence a problem for Derek?

2. Brian faces difficult situations in *Hatchet*, *The River*, and *Brian's Winter*. How are the situations similar in each book? In what way are they different? What do these situations reveal about Brian's character as he grows and changes in each book?

3. In *Hatchet* Brian has vivid dreams, and in *The River* he has hallucinations. What does Brian learn about himself and his situation through these dreams and hallucinations? How are they similar? How are they different?

4. How does Brian divide his time in the wilderness in both *Hatchet* and *Brian's Winter*? Why does he use this method instead of using months, days, hours, and minutes?

5. Each of the characters in these three novels—Brian, as well as Derek Holtzer in *The River*—undergoes a learning experience. What roles do nature and animals play in each of the experiences Brian and Derek have?

6. *Brian's Winter* was written at the request of Paulsen's readers who wondered what might have happened if Brian hadn't been rescued, and had been left to face a harsh, northern winter. In what ways, however, does winter make things easier for Brian?

7. Do you think Gary Paulsen would have been able to write *Hatchet*, *The River*, and *Brian's Winter* if he had not undergone similar experiences in the wilderness? Why or why not? What do you think Paulsen's first-hand experience in the wilderness adds to his books?

Answer Key

Page 14

1. Until Gary Paulsen observed the wolves hunting and killing the doe, he believed that every story in the woods had a happy ending and that nothing ever really got hurt. The wolf hunt helped him understand that animals are not right or wrong—they just are. Wolves don't know they are wolves. **2.** Some friends gave Paulsen four older dogs and a broken sled. Paulsen was trapping beavers for the state of Minnesota to earn some money, and he used the dog team to check his trap lines. **3.** When Paulsen observes the "joke" that Columbia plays on Obeah, he realizes the complicated thinking behind it and it sets off a chain reaction in his mind. He feels that any animal might do what Columbia did, and he can no longer trap animals. His three lessons in "blood"—the doe's, Storm's, and his own—help him realize how little he knows about animal behavior. **4.** Answers will vary. Some students may choose Olaf because he is very strong and aggressive, while others may choose Columbia because he is very smart. **5.** People use controlled fire and animals do not. **6.** Scarhead had an opportunity to kill Paulsen, but he did not. Scarhead taught Paulsen that it is wrong to throw sticks at 400-pound bears, and that Paulsen is nothing more or less than any other animal in the woods. **7.** Paulsen finds some grouse eggs and places them in Hawk's nest. When the baby grouse hatch and begin to fly around the yard, Hawk sits on top of the woodpile in the yard and attacks anything she feels might threaten the chicks. **8.** Answers could include: Paulsen sees a red squirrel—not usually a carnivorous animal—kill and eat a chipmunk. He sees a strange green-yellow light ebb and flow in the woods during a night run. A fox takes a grouse in the snow and does not leave any tracks. A group of cedar waxwings settle on tree limbs in groups of eight or ten birds and pass berries to each other until every bird on the limb has one. A fawn touches the outstretched hand of a young boy with its nose. A deer, frozen solid, stands upright in the middle of the trail.

Page 15

1. When Paulsen insists on going the wrong way, Cookie takes the team over the edge of a large drop. Then the dogs refuse to run for Paulsen until the next morning. From this experience, Paulsen learns not to challenge the team and to trust their instincts. **2.** Storm used the sticks he carried as a way to communicate with Paulsen, and to let Paulsen know he was doing the right thing. **3.** He is ill with a high fever and delirium sets in. **4.** He sees the Iditarod as something basic and elemental in a world controlled by technology. At the end of the race he actually stops and cannot bring himself to cross the finish line. He does not want the race to end. **5.** The dogs blow out of the chute so hard that Paulsen's arms are nearly jerked out of their sockets. When they sweep around a turn he loses control of the sled. **6.** There is no snow for the sled runners, and many dead tree stumps, the result of a forest fire, litter the trail. **7.** Some of the people Paulsen "meets" are Eskimos, who help him and his dogs when they have problems. Others, like the man in the trenchcoat, do not help Paulsen and hinder his progress. **8.** Answers may vary but could include the beginning of the race, when Paulsen goes 40 or 50 miles out of his way and then turns back, becoming entangled with the 27 teams that were following his lead.

Page 16

Sample answers are given.

1. Cause: Paulsen lights a fire after a day's run with a team of young sled dogs. **Effect on Plot:** The dogs are afraid of the fire and lunge against their chains. **Effect on Gary Paulsen:** Paulsen watches as the dogs lose their fear and wonders if people would have gone through this process as quickly. He gains new respect for the dogs' intelligence. **2. Cause:** Paulsen throws a stick at Scarhead the bear when the animal comes in the family compound looking for food. **Effect on Plot:** Scarhead looms over Paulsen and threatens to kill him, but then backs down. **Effect on Gary Paulsen:** Paulsen realizes he is nothing more or less than any other animal in the woods. **3. Cause:** The State of Minnesota pays a bounty for beavers because the animals are running amuck, flooding highways and pastures. **Effect on Plot:** A friend gives Paulsen four sled dogs to help him set his trap lines for beavers. **Effect on Gary Paulsen:** Paulsen begins to learn how to raise and run sled dogs. **4. Cause:** Paulsen and his sled dogs begin to climb the Alaska Range during the Iditarod. **Effect on Plot:** The team has crossed the highest mountain range in North America. **Effect on Gary Paulsen:** Paulsen feels he is becoming a true human, before we became cluttered by civilization, and doesn't care now if he wins the race.

Page 17

Sample answers are given.

Beginning of the Book 1. The State of Minnesota; in the deep woods found in the northern part of the state. **2.** A beautiful early winter morning; bright sun; temperature ten below; a frozen lake; willow trees and brush all around. **3.** A deer explodes out of the woods ahead of a pack of wolves. She bounds out onto the bad ice, but since it is early winter, it cannot hold her. She falls through the ice, climbs out, but loses her lead on the wolves and they catch her. **4.** Paulsen is struck by the beauty of early winter in this part of the woods. He describes himself as "dancing with winter," and recalls an ancient Navajo prayer. But then he witnesses the wolves killing the doe, and he comes to realize that he wants to know more about the animals in the woods. **End of the Book 1.** Anchorage; the staging area on Fourth Street at the beginning of the Iditarod. **2.** Winter; the snow is shallow; close to dark. **3.** Because the snow is shallow the sleds cut through to bare asphalt, there is no way to steer the sleds and keep control. **4.** The dogs blow out of the chutes. Paulsen has a hard time keeping control of the sled due to the shallow snow. He rolls over and slides out of downtown Anchorage on his face.

Page 23

1. Russel's father is coughing because he smokes cigarettes, and Russel feels that tobacco is not a part of Eskimo culture. **2.** He knows that something is bothering Russel, and he thinks Oogruk's knowledge of the old ways might help Russel. **3.** Missionaries came and told the Eskimos that singing and dancing were wrong. **4.** Russel has respect for his father and for Oogruk, but he feels he can learn more from Oogruk. Russel's father has abandoned many of the old ways, and Russel doesn't feel he can describe to his father why he feels unhappy with himself. **5.** Russel learns that in some ways dogs are smarter than people. When he gets lost, he gives the dogs his lead, and they instinctively take Russel in the direction of home. **6.** His father approves, and most people in the village feel that Russel is old enough to know what he is doing. **7.** Answers will vary, but students should point out that Oogruk says an old man knows when death is coming, and he should be left alone. Oogruk wants to die in the old Eskimo way, and Russel does the right thing by respecting his wishes. **8.** As Oogruk says, Russel must see the country and find himself in the old Eskimo tradition. Russel must run with the dogs and become "what the dogs will help you become."

Page 24

1. Russel is upset. He does not want to see anybody, especially somebody on a snow machine. He feels the idea of a snow machine is out of place in the wilderness. **2.** Answers should include that the young girl resembles the woman in Russel's dream, and for this reason he does not mind taking her along with him. **3.** The people and the animals in *Dogsong* respect one another. They understand when it is their time to die. In "The Dream," the mammoth understands it must die to provide meat for the man, and the villagers feel deeply for the plight of the mammoth and thank the beast for the meat it provides. **4.** He learns that the bear is the same as the mammoth, and he sets the shaft of the lance in the ground. Unlike the dream, however, the bear doesn't accept death and hits Russel with a stunning blow. **5.** Nancy became very upset and screamed for Russel to take the baby away. Russel felt a "tearing sadness" because there was no life in the baby. It was born dead. **6.** Answers will vary but should include that Russel was trying to reconnect with the ancient ways of his ancestors, hunting and using methods that existed before technology was introduced. He found what he was looking for—he hunted successfully, survived the cold, and rescued a young Eskimo girl. **7.** In the open wilderness of the Arctic, Russel learns that without his dogs he would die. He was nothing without his dogs. Together they form one single intelligence, battling the cold and the wind.

Page 25

1. He is confused. He uses a snow machine and owns a motorsled, but doesn't like to use them. He is not happy with himself, but is not sure why. **2.** Russel says he has a feeling like being alive. The sled flew across the ice and Russel felt he was alive with the sled and the ice and the snow. **3.** He becomes both the mammoth and the hunter in his dream. He finds his song during the mammoth hunt, and understands the cycle of life and death for both people and animals in the Arctic tundra. **4.** Russel would not have understood the importance of the sled dogs Oogruk owned nor of what it was like to be part of a sled team, surviving on his own in the wilderness. **Best theme statement:** It isn't the destination that counts, it's what you learn on the journey.

Page 26

Sample answers are given.
A Character Trait of Russel: Caring. **What Russel Thinks:** After Oogruk dies, Russel thinks of going back to the sled and getting the small harpoon to place in Oogruk's lap. **What Russel Feels:** A tearing sadness when Nancy gives birth to a lifeless baby. **What Russel Does:** He goes back for Oogruk after the old man tells Russel to leave him alone on the sea ice. **What Russel Says:** Russel goes back to Nancy with food and tells her, "I said I would be back."

Page 33

1. Brian's parents have separated and are planning to divorce. **2.** He remembers seeing his mother in a station wagon with a strange man. **3.** He hears small sounds—the hum of insects, hisses, birds singing, splashes from fish jumping. It is a "hissing pulse sound," very different from the traffic sounds in the city. **4.** Both Gary Paulsen and Russel plan to be in the wilderness and are prepared for some of the dangers and harsh weather they may face. Brian did not plan to be in the wilderness and has no experience living in nature. **5.** All the small sounds of the wilderness suddenly cease. The insects and animals are startled by Brian's voice, and for the first time in his life Brian hears total silence. **6.** Brian has a fingernail clipper, a billfold, a hatchet, a broken digital watch, and the clothes he is wearing. Brian himself is his most valuable asset, however. If he keeps a clear head, he can think of ways to use each of these assets to his best advantage. **7.** Brian understands and accepts that the bear does not want to hurt him. He learns that baseless fear is unhelpful for survival. **8.** The shower of sparks that result after Brian throws a hatchet at a porcupine and hits the cave wall convince him that he needs—and can make—a fire.

Page 34

1. He had been depressed before, but now that he has fire and food he is more hopeful. He finds that when he is busy, he is less depressed. **2.** He watches the kingfisher catch a small fish in the lake, and he realizes that fish can also be a food source for him. **3.** He knows that the plane had come as far off to the side of the flight plan as the pilot thought they would have to come. Brian feels they will not return, and that he will not be able to make it if they do not come back for him soon. **4.** Brian feels afraid only for a moment. He nods to the wolf and realizes that, like him, the wolf is another part of the woods. **5.** He learns to look for the outline of the bird, to see the shape instead of the feathers or color. He realizes that patience is everything—waiting and thinking and doing things right. **6.** For all this time, the hatchet had been everything to Brian. Without the hatchet, he had no fire, no tools, no weapon. He also gets very angry at himself, because his carelessness in losing the hatchet was, he felt, something he would have done when he first arrived. **7.** Brian has gained immensely in his ability to observe what is happening and react to it. He has also become more thoughtful; he thinks slowly before speaking. Food never loses its wonder for him.

Page 35

Solution: Brian remembers a survival show he saw in which a woman found beans on a bush in the desert and used them to make a stew. He realizes that in the north woods, there must be berry bushes. **Problem:** A skunk comes into Brian's shelter and eats from his store of turtle eggs. The skunk sprays Brian, blinding him temporarily, and he realizes that food has to be protected. **Solution:** Brian realizes he needs something to spring the spear forward, some way to make it move faster than the fish. He decides to make a bow and arrow. **Problem:** Fish were not something he could store if they were dead. **Solution:** To get to the plane, Brian would need a raft. The shore of the lake is littered with driftwood, and Brian uses the limbs of the logs to weave them together into a raft.

Page 36

1. Fear and horror. 2. Answers could include details of the pilot's condition or of Brian becoming entangled in the birdcage of formers and cables. 3. Sadness and depression. 4. Answers could include other misfortunes that had befallen Brian, such as his injuries from the crash, his sickness following his meal of gut cherries, and the mosquitoes.

Page 42

1. They work for a government survival school. They want Brian to return to the wilderness so they can record what he does and then teach others how to survive with more accuracy. 2. Brian cannot walk through a park without watching the trees for game. He sees and hears everything around him—colors, movement, noise. 3. Brian says that Derek wants to learn how to survive in the wilderness, but if he unloads all the gear he has brought with him, it won't be a real survival situation—it will just be a game. 4. He becomes aware of everything going on around him. He knows instantly that it will rain that evening. He hears each bird and locates it. He smells the air and can tell that there aren't any animals in the immediate area. 5. Brian falls off the edge of a hill when the soft soil doesn't hold him. When he pushes himself up, he notices the rocks around him near the lake. One of the black stones is flint, which Brian can use to make fire.
6. Brian tells Derek he thinks you can tell people what to do, but that doesn't teach them how to live or how to do it. He feels that you'd have to bring each person to the wilderness, drop him or her in the lake, and let the person swim out and try to live. 7. A sharp crack of thunder wakes Brian and sends him to the back of the shelter. Derek is trying to use the radio when it is struck by lightning, and he falls into a coma. 8. He feels helpless, just as he did when he was alone right after the crash.

Page 43

1. Since Derek is in a coma and defenseless, Brian is afraid that wild animals might come and attack him. 2. Brian finds that by frantically paddling through each curve in the river, he can keep the raft moving almost at the speed of the current and away from any brush or snags on the sides of the river. 3. Brian hallucinates due to a lack of sleep. He imagines that there is someone on the raft who will help him. 4. Brian has successfully steered the raft during the night and has stayed on course. The possibility of a waterfall is a turning point because it presents Brian's worst problem on the river. Once he overcomes it, he feels more confident that he will reach help.
5. Brian is thrown from the raft into the water. Derek remains on the raft because Brian has tied him onto it, but the raft disappears down the river and Brian must find it. 6. A small boy and his dog spot Brian and Derek as the raft drifts by a dock. The boy goes for help. 7. Derek comes out of the coma in one week and is fully recovered in six months. 8. Brian feels that after two experiences in the wilderness he is more qualified to be in the woods than most people.

Page 44

Title/Author: *The River*/Gary Paulsen **Characters:** Brian Robeson, Derek Holtzer, Brian's mother, Bill Mannerly, Erik Ballard **Setting:** A lake and river in the Canadian wilderness. **Problem:** A lightning bolt from a violent thunderstorm sends Derek into a coma and short-circuits the radio. Brian knows that Derek had just completed his weekly check-in, and no one will come looking for them right away. Yet he must get Derek to a doctor. **Event 1:** Brian looks at Derek's map and sees that a trading post is 100 miles away upriver. **Event 2:** Brian uses poplar trees felled by beavers to make a raft. **Event 3:** Brian begins to hallucinate after losing sleep for so many days. **Event 4:** Brian is thrown from the raft and loses Derek when they hit rapids. **Event 5:** Brian finds Derek, still on the raft, after nearly drowning in the rapids. **Solution:** Brian and Derek reach a dock on the river where a young boy sees them and gets help.

Sample summary is given.
The government asks Brian if he will go back into the wilderness, so that astronauts and the military can learn the survival tactics that kept him alive. Brian will be accompanied by a government psychologist, Derek Holtzer, who will watch what he does and take notes. During a storm, Derek is hit by lightning, and falls into a coma. Brian discovers the radio is dead, and he is afraid to leave Derek alone and go for help. He builds a raft, and carries Derek a hundred miles down a river to a trading post, where they are rescued.

Page 45
1. the mud held his arm, seemed to pull at him, tried to take him down/personification **2.** the small monsters trying to bleed him dry/metaphor **3.** Like a camera taking pictures with a strobe light/simile **4.** They hit it off/idiom **5.** flicker of new flame/alliteration **6.** images frozen in the split instants of brilliance/sensory words **7.** A whooshing—water/onomatopoeia

Page 51
1. Brian feels the food has softened him, making him think of the city and hamburgers and malts instead of the situation in the woods. **2.** Brian has forgotten the primary rule of surviving in the wilderness: Always pay attention to what is happening. He has missed the warnings that summer is ending. **3.** The geese wake Brian up, and they are a reminder to him that sleeping does not get things done. A week of cold rain reminds him how poor he is if he cannot look for food daily. **4.** He wishes them a good hunt, thinking to himself that a good hunt is everything. Just after the crash, the howling of the wolves might have given Brian an eerie feeling, but now he looks upon the wolves as fellow predators. **5.** Brian takes a portion of the doe the wolves have killed, and has more food than he has ever had before. **6.** Because of all the meat from the doe, Brian does not have to hunt for over a week. He decides that going after larger game makes more sense in the coming winter. **7.** When a bear invades Brian's shelter looking for food, Betty sprays the bear and saves Brian's life. **8.** Brian had never seen anything so clean. More than that, Brian is inside the snowy scene, and the beauty of it becomes a part of him. **9.** He sees many animal tracks in the freshly fallen snow.

Page 52
1. He feels good because he has food that will allow him to live, but he also feels bad because he has ended the life of an animal in the woods. **2.** She has gone into hibernation for the winter. **3.** He watches a rabbit run on top of the snow without sinking. **4.** Brian sees the hatchet as being the key to it all. He would not have been able to make a shelter and weapons without the hatchet. **5.** Brian hears a sharp, blistering crack of sound when he is half asleep. What Brian

thinks are gunshots turn out to be exploding trees. In the extreme cold, the sap freezes inside the trees and expands. The pressure inside the tree causes an explosion. **6.** Brian had been settling into the shelter, and not paying attention to things. With the snowshoes he felt like moving and doing things again. **7.** Brian had thought killing with arrows was bad and slow, but the wolf kill seemed to take forever. He wondered how nature could let an animal suffer the way the moose had suffered. **8.** Brian knew it was too warm for trees to explode. **9.** The woods had become a part of Brian's life. The heat of it seemed to match his pulse and his breathing.

Page 53
1. Before: A large bear smells the odor from Brian's cooking pot. **After:** The bear rips the entire log side of the shelter and then flings Brian 20 feet, end over end. **2. Before:** Brian opens the door of his shelter and discovers that the world is white—the woods are covered with the first snowfall of winter. **After:** Because the snow is new, his clothing kept him warm, and he had never hunted in the snow before, Brian decides to go hunting and finds a moose. **3. Before:** Brian moves out from his shelter in gradual circles to explore the winter woods, and he witnesses a wolf kill. **After:** Now that he has snowshoes and is mobile, Brian decides to investigate the source of the popping sounds.

Page 54
Sample answers are given.

Story Details: Brian feeds a skunk outside his shelter. When it disappears around a large boulder, Brian follows the skunk to find out where it is going.

Details About Character: Brian feels a kinship with the animals in the wilderness. He feels he is just another animal in the woods.

Character's Thoughts or Dialogue: "You're living here? You've moved in on me?" "Wonderful—I've got a roommate with a terminal hygiene problem."

Tone: Amusing